Disaster Planning Guide

What To Do Before, During, And After Disasters

By

Paolo Jose de Luna

Paolo Jose De Luna

The information provided herein is stated to be truthful and consistent, in that any liability, in terms of inattention or otherwise, by any usage or abuse of any policies, processes, or directions contained within is the solitary and utter responsibility of the recipient reader. Under no circumstances will any legal responsibility or blame be held against the publisher for any reparation, damages, or monetary loss due to the information herein, either directly or indirectly.

Respective authors own all copyrights not held by the publisher.

Paolo Jose De Luna

The information herein is offered for informational purposes solely, and is universal as so. The presentation of the information is without contract or any type of guarantee assurance.

The trademarks that are used are without any consent, and the publication of the trademark is without permission or backing by the trademark owner. All trademarks and brands within this book are for clarifying purposes only and are the owned by the owners themselves, not affiliated with this document.

Table of Contents

INTRODUCTION

From house fires up to earthquakes, tsunamis, and flash floods, there's no telling what these disasters can do to us and when they occur. They put lives at risk and they damage properties from thousands up to millions of dollars in the damage they wrought.

Disasters can occur at any place, any time, and to anyone. No one has the ability to predict when and where these disasters will occur. And that's why the best measure that you can do is to prepare for them.

As you may already have known, preparation is always stressed out in a variety of guides and disaster management plans. However, these so-called "plans" are easily thrown out of the box when the disasters truly strike. What makes these plans so flawed and confusing that a lot of people just end up panicking? Well, that's because most guides on disaster just make up generic preparation measures without having any specific details on each one.

If you're going to prepare for a disaster, you need a thorough and concrete plan that you can use to prepare. May it be for a fire or for a flood, you need to know on what to do to protect your family, your friends, and your loved ones. You also need to minimize the damage to your home and to save whatever you can in order to move on after the disaster has struck.

But aside from the preparation phase for a disaster, you also need to know on what to do during the disaster itself. Will you give in to the fear while a fire rages on or if you're stranded on your home's roof while an intense storm has caused immense levels of floods? Or will you compose yourself and follow the steps that you need to do in order to survive the disaster, as well as protecting other people? That's ultimately up to you.

And then, there's the post-disaster measures that you need to do. Most people often get confused on what to do in order to recover after a disaster has struck. A lot of people just end up crying or moping after everything that they've owned has been destroyed or worse, their homes have been wrecked apart after a hurricane. But are those really the things that you should think about right at this moment? Will you just stand there and wallow in despair or will you stand up and fight in order to get back what you've lost?

In this book, you'll be learning on how to deal with disasters. Right from the beginning, you'll learn on how to properly prepare for a disaster, what are the things that you need to prepare, what to do during a disaster, and up to what to do in order to rest, recover, and recuperate after the disaster has subsided.

In order for you to survive a disaster, you need to be prepared, not just before a disaster, but for all three of these phases. You'll be presented with various facts about disasters and disaster management, as well as real life scenarios that you can utilize in order to survive various kinds of disasters like house fires, floods, tsunamis, earthquakes, blizzards, blackouts, and more.

Chapter 1 - What are Disasters?

Photo credit: Dutourdumonde Photography / Shutterstock.com

By definition, a disaster is a sudden event that often results in a catastrophe, loss of life, and destruction of property. Oftentimes, disasters call upon the services of various government and non-government organizations to assist civilians in evacuation, containment of the disaster, limiting damage to property, saving the wildlife, and prevent the loss of life.

With the number of organizations working together, a state of calamity or emergency is usually called upon in a particular location where the disaster has occurred in order to make use of the emergency disaster funds that the government has set aside especially for times like this.

Disasters can be divided into two main categories: natural disasters and man-made disasters.

Natural disasters are composed of (you've guessed it) natural phenomenon caused by Mother Nature or the natural flow of the world that result in the loss of life or destruction of property which would include disasters like volcanic eruptions, earthquakes, avalanches, landslides, the appearance of sinkholes, blizzards, tornadoes, wildfires, and the like. Geographical and meteorological organizations are primarily the ones who are responsible in predicting the occurrence of these natural disasters, but the fact is that there is no perfect and flawless way in detecting when and where these disasters will occur. But with the use of the empirical evidence that these scientists and researchers gather, time is given to the people in order to prepare or evacuate before these natural disasters occur.

Man-made disasters, on the other hand, result from the anthropogenic hazards that are made by humans which include disasters like chemical spills, radiation spills, nuclear explosions, blackouts, cybernetic attacks, the use of biological and chemical weapons, explosions, civil unrest, terrorist attacks, and the like. It is often that historical landmarks and crowded locations are made targets by certain groups which result in man-made disasters, affecting hundreds to thousands of lives which can lead to damage to property, civilian unrest, widespread panic, injuries, or even death. Man-made disasters are artificial in nature, often involving the use of technology or through the influence of a person or object on society which causes massive unrest or panic throughout the people.

Another type of disaster that can be correlated with man-made disasters is accidents. While man-made in nature, accidents are through the *accidental* action coming from human beings. Other man-made disasters can be caused by deliberate action, hence they can be classified in a different classification. There are a number of accidents that can turn into disasters such as road accidents, railway accidents, maritime accidents, nuclear accidents, even space accidents, and more.

No matter what kind of disaster, however, results in unrest, property damage, and the loss of life. Therefore, it's important to know when and how to prepare for each and every kind of disaster. While you may be overwhelmed by this thought, the answer would be a big and resounding "Yes". You can definitely prepare for each disaster – all you have to do is have a clear and calm mind, along with sound judgment based on empirical evidence proven by scientific and tested measures.

The measures in preparing for disasters require the knowledge, the skills, and the dedication in

Natural Disasters

Natural disasters are brought upon by Mother Nature and almost entirely, there's no absolute way to stop them.

These disasters often bring about an enormous amount of death and destruction in their wakes because of the size and the scale that each type of natural disaster can cause.

Natural disasters include the following:

- Earthquakes
- Wildfires
- Avalanches
- Landslides
- Sinkholes
- Volcanic eruptions
- Blizzards
- Drought
- Flooding
- Tornadoes
- Cyclones
- Hurricanes
- Heat waves

- Maelstroms
- Water spouts
- Hailstorms

While natural disasters are generally caused by the forces of Mother Nature, there are some human factors that contribute to the development of some of these disasters. For example, improper waste disposal that leads to clogging up of the sewer systems can contribute to the development of flooding in a particular area or illegal logging in mountainous areas can lead to landslides towards the lower lying plains.

Man-Made Disasters

Man-made disasters come from direct or indirect human intervention that lead to a catastrophic loss of life and destruction of property. Compared to the natural causes of natural disasters, man-made disasters result from the actions of human beings, either intended or unintended, which result in a variety of disasters. Man-made disasters often vary in scale, ranging from a small but damaging disaster up to a large-scale man-made disaster that can affect up to millions or even billions of people at one time.

Man-made disasters include the following:

- Oil spills
- Radiation poisoning
- Nuclear fallout
- Wars
- Chemical spills
- Civil unrest and riots

- Road accidents
- Railway accidents
- Maritime accidents
- Aircraft accidents
- Structural and industrial related disasters
- Diseases
- Terrorist attacks

Because of the presence of human intervention, man-made disasters can happen more frequently compared to natural disasters. And because of their nature and the ability to predict its occurrence, there are also a number of ways on how to prevent man-made disasters from happening. For example, measures in the police and national security forces in some countries have been improved to prevent riots from occurring or prevent them from worsening to a graver extent.

Chapter 2 - Preparing for Disasters

Photo credit: Nils Versemann / Shutterstock.com

After getting to know the different kinds of disasters, it's time to know how to properly prepare for a disaster. Sure, there might be no way that you can tell when, how, and what kind of disaster that you might encounter in the future.

However, that's the thing about these disasters – you never know what, when, and where they'll happen. That's why you need to be prepared just in case so you don't get hurt or lose your life or your limb.

Starting off this guide, you need to be equipped with the proper knowledge and a particular set of skills so that you won't get hurt and you won't lose your valuables when a disaster strikes. Here are the things that you should remember when you're preparing before a disaster even hits you and your home.

Disaster Preparedness Plan

During the last five years, we've suffered from typhoons, hurricanes, earthquakes, and all sorts of disasters that sent most of us in a fit of panic. However, there's more to disaster preparedness than just knowing what to do during a disaster. The preparation phase for a disaster is equally important which puts a bigger issue in question – are you really prepared for a disaster?

Before you start heading off face first into the brunt of a disaster, you need to be first equipped with the proper knowledge, skills, and attitude when it comes to facing disasters. Your first and best weapon against any kind of disaster isn't a big fire axe or a rubber raft. It's your cunning, intellect, and resourcefulness that will be saving your life and the lives of other people in dire times.

Establish your very own disaster preparedness plan by creating a list of things to do and things to bring along when a disaster strikes. It doesn't have to be a long list. In fact, the more concise, the better the list. This will help in summarizing what you need to do during a disaster and even improve your situation when a disaster strikes by allowing you to prepare things beforehand.

Keeping Your Documents

It's always a good idea to keep all your important documents in a safe and secure place. This would include your birth certificates, your marriage certificates, copies of certain contracts, passports, security cards,deeds, important receipts especially if they carry warranty, IDs, medical records, and more. It's going to be a pain if you lose them since most of these documents are difficult to acquire and losing them makes it even harder. Keeping them secured in one place or storage that you can immediately grab in one go will be helpful when you need to evacuate your home. This would also be best if your documents are kept in a strong box that's resistant from both fire, moisture, and trauma. If you can, you should also secure a digital copy of these documents for safe measure.

Storing Food and Water

When it comes to preparing for any kind of disaster, you have to make sure that you've stored enough food and water.

This prepares you for any situation wherein you don't have access to food, you've run out of your conventional supply of food from your home, or you've lost the means to acquire food and food products due to the effects of the disaster. Canned foods and preserved foods work best for long term storage since they last quite a long time before they expire. Stock up on nutritious and well-preserved foods like canned meat, fish, seafood, vegetables, fruits, beans, and more. They're easy to get and they're a lot easier to eat, all you have to do is pop open the container and munch away. Sure, there might be some risks involved in eating food directly out from cans, but heating them up won't be too hard if you have enough means and supplies to start a fire without a stove. It's hard to cope with searching for food to eat during and after a disaster when food supply is scarce and hard to come by.

Your Emergency Bug OutBag

When the time comes that you need to leave your home because it's no longer safe, you won't have time to pack your things. This brings us to the next case wherein you should pack up your emergency disaster bag that contains all your essentials including food, medical supplies, documents, some cash, extra clothes, clean drinking water, an emergency radio, a flashlight, and other emergency supplies that you may need during your evacuation. This lets you save time when disaster comes and you won't need to worry leaving anything important once you bug out of your home.

Know Your Escape Routes

If the time comes when you really have to leave the safety of your own home, it's safe to assume that you already have an idea on where to go and how you'll get there. If you don't, well, you're probably in a huge pinch. During a disaster, public or even private transportation may be crippled because of the effects of the disaster like hurricanes, floods, blizzards, massive earthquakes, and tsunamis. Aside from that, you need to establish escape routes throughout the house to ensure that you safely leave your house when your own home becomes a potential deathtrap for you and your family. And it's not just your house; you should also implement this in your workplace where people have a higher chance to panic and block all the conventional exit routes. Know the fastest and the safest way out of your home or your workplace in cases of fires or even when a burglar raids your home and practice getting through it so you don't fumble and mess things up during a real life situation.

Plan Out Your Meeting Place

It's difficult to gather your family members, loved ones, and friends all in one location when a disaster strikes. This is especially true when a disaster reaches a destructive capacity that it affects people on a national scale. Another part of your disaster preparedness should be deciding on where you and your loved ones should meet in the event that you are separated in disaster. It should be a place that's safe, secure, familiar, and free from danger to serve as your shelter. Having a meeting place during and after a disaster is a great way to reunite with your loved ones and erase the worries and paranoia that disasters bring once family members and loved ones are separated from each other. Good meeting places include public parks, churches, evacuation centers, schools, and even a home of a friend or relative that's particularly safe from a disaster epicenter.

And there you have it – preparing for a disaster may be a tedious task at first glance, but once a disaster hits, you'll probably wish that you've done it beforehand. So why wait until a blizzard or a typhoon hits? Get off your couch and start preparing for a disaster *now*! You'll save time, money, and the lives of your loves ones with these seemingly minor preparations.

Chapter 3 - What to Do During Disasters

Photo credit: Lakeview Images / Shutterstock.com

More often than not, a lot of people tend to panic and feel like their pants are set on fire during a disaster. That's not just because of the disaster itself, but it's the effects if the disaster that puts us in an anxious state. But you shouldn't let anxiety and fear overcome your mind. Instead, you need to have a sound and composed mindset in order to make sharp decisions that can save you and your loved ones during a disaster.

After getting to familiarize yourself with the disaster preparedness phase, it's time to go into the action-oriented approach. It's time to know what you should do *during* a disaster. In this chapter, we'll be discussing on the things that you should do during a particular disaster situation so that you can evacuate safe and sound either alone or with your loved ones. With the proper knowledge and the appropriate set of skills, you can keep yourself and everyone around you safe by following these steps.

Fires

Fires are a very common type of disaster that can occur in your home or in any commercial establishment. It can happen at work, at school, or at home. The usual causes of fires include an unattended candle, leaking gas pipes, broken stoves, or accidentally lit combustible fuel sources. But because it's so common, there are a lot of measures that you can take during a fire.

- If you're in a building that's on fire, make sure that you stay low by crouching on the floor. Smoke rises which makes it harder to breathe when you're standing up. If you go below your waistline, breathing will be a lot easier and you won't be inhaling all the toxic substances that the smoke carries. If the fire grows even more intense and the amount of smoke makes it thicker and harder to breathe, crawl on the floor if you have to.

- Once you hear the fire alarm sound, get moving. No use in standing around and waiting for the fire to spread. You may only have a few seconds of getting out of the building, so move fast.

- Make sure that you follow the fire escape routes of a building to ensure that you won't get stuck in dead ends. Most often, people die from suffocation or get burned alive because they don't follow the conventional escape routes during a fire due to their panicking which gets them trapped in a room.

- If you see a door with smoke coming out of it, find another escape route. This will tell you that the room on the other side has the fires spread far and opening the door will just let more smoke come in and help in spreading the fire even further.

- If you need to open a door, do it slowly and securely. When a room is filled with smoke and heat, pressure builds up which pushes against the door. At times, the smoke or the air may cause a blow back so strong that it can fling a door out of its hinges and across the room.

- If you get your clothes on fire, be sure to stop, drop, and roll. Cover your face with your hands and it's best to smother the fire with a wet blanket or towel. If you do get burned, treat the burned area with water and cover it with a damp cloth. Once you're out of the fire, be sure to get medical attention immediately.

- If there are any people or pets trapped inside the building, make sure that you tell the firefighters immediately. You don't need to be the hero who charges into the building himself to save someone's life.

Earthquakes

Falling next to house fires, earthquakes are also a common disaster felt all around the world. Earthquakes happen due to two reasons – when the tectonic plates on the Earth's crust moves or when a volcanic activity below the earth causes a disturbance that reaches the geographical stability of the surface. Because of this, there's no way in telling when and where earthquakes will occur in the future, but there are instruments that can tell when they might happen on an immediate basis. With the short amount of time that you can prepare for an earthquake, knowing what to do during this disaster would be a lot more helpful. Here are some of the things that you should do during an earthquake.

- When an earthquake occurs, stay where you are. If you're indoors, stay indoors. If you're outdoors, stay outdoors. The biggest danger during an earthquake are falling objects that may hit you. It's dangerous to run around during an earthquake where there are falling debris and when you're balance is at a total mess.

- DROP, COVER, and HOLD ON – these are the main strategies for you to use to survive an earthquake. Drop to the floor and onto your hands and knees to protect yourself from debris while still being able to move, start to cover your head and neck with your hands and arms to protect yourself from falling debris like glass, concrete, wood, furniture, and appliances, and hold on to a safe area where you can take shelter until the earthquake finally subsides.

- Find a safe and sturdy place where you can shelter yourself. Stay under a table, a desk, or even just the corner of the doorway. Make sure you steer clear from cabinets, glass windows, light fixtures, furniture, or anything that can fall on you. The kitchen is considered to be one of the most dangerous places to be in when an earthquake occurs because of all the things that can potentially fall on you. So stay clear away from potentially fall-risk objects.

- DO NOT USE THE ELEVATOR. This is quite self-explanatory but there are still some people who end up getting stuck or even dying in an elevator during an earthquake. The power may go out during an earthquake and the elevator may go haywire, potentially cutting the steel wires holding it together, making it a deathtrap during an earthquake.

- If you're outdoors and you're driving, get your car out of traffic and move it aside. Stay away from bridges as these may crumble and some debris may fall on you. Also stay away from lampposts, buildings, and poles since these can fall on you and your car.

- If you're stuck in a crowded location, don't panic and immediately rush to the exit. Instead, stay calm and get to cover as this is the most effective way to stay safe and uninjured.

- If you're near the sea or ocean when the earthquake occurs, get to higher ground immediately. Get away from the body of water as far and as fast as you can since a tsunami may occur. Listen to the local tsunami warning system when an earthquake's epicenter is located in the middle of the sea.

- If you're out in the mountains, be sure to stay away from trees as they have a high risk of falling. Also watch for any signs of potential landslides in the area. Be sure to steer clear from any of these areas. As much as possible, look for an open area where you can protect yourself from falling objects like trees, rocks, and branches.

- Don't light candles or lighters to serve as a light source. Earthquakes can damage gas pipelines and may serve as a flammable source that can spark a huge fire if you're not careful.

Hurricanes

Next up is hurricanes. These are tropical super storms or cyclones that contain an immense amount of rainfall and possess incredibly strong winds that can lift things as heavy as cars flying off the ground. Hurricanes can be monitored with the help of weather stations that watch its course and movement. If you're in an area where hurricanes are common, here are the things that you should do during a hurricane.

- Listen to the hurricane warnings and guidelines on the radio. Be aware on the progress of the hurricane with the help of your local news. Since power may be out during a hurricane, it would be handy to have a battery powered radio to help you keep up to track with the progress and course of the hurricane.

- Be sure to secure your home by bringing in outdoor furniture indoors, closing the shutters, securing the doors and windows, and setting up storm barricades if you need to.

- If you need to, turn off the power to your home. When a hurricane arrives, power outages are common and it's actually a risk for you if you keep your electricity running because of the danger from live wires and broken power lines during the storm.

- Turn off all your gas pipes and your propane tanks. These can get damaged during the storm and may pose a risk of starting a fire or a chemical leak in your home.

- Evacuate your home if the local authorities announce that it has become too dangerous in your area. If you live in a mobile home, a high rise building, or near the coast, you are at the greatest risk of taking the brunt of the hurricane. Should you feel that you are in danger, you should also evacuate your home or anywhere you may find yourself during the storm.

- During a hurricane, always stay indoors and stay away from glass windows and doors.

- Close, secure, and brace all of your doors and windows at home. These may be forced open by the sheer strength of the winds if you don't close them properly. Even if you feel like the storm has passed, keep your doors and windows closed. This may just be the eye of the hurricane where the winds subside – it will pick up again once the eye of the storm has passed through your area.

- Go to the safest room in your home like a bathroom where you can take shelter. If you have a small interior room on the lowest level of your house that contains all your emergency rations and supplies, it would be best to stay there for the remainder of the storm.

Flooding

During a hurricane, your primary enemy is the wind speed of the storm. However, when it comes to flooding, your enemy is the rainfall quantity – the water. During a flood, the water levels rise beyond the manageable level and most often, evacuation is necessary, especially for those who live in the low-lying areas. If you're in an area that may be at risk of flooding, here are the things that you should do during a flood.

- Monitor your surroundings and listen to the announcements of your local news team. If you have a radio, always keep in check on the areas affected by the floods and the level of the water. This is crucial in terms of when and where to evacuate when the time comes.

- Avoid driving if you can. The streets will most probably be flooded and your car will get jammed if you try to force your way through. Be sure to stock up on supplies before the storm even hits your area.

- Get to higher ground. Since the water levels may rise even further, it would be safer for you and your family to stay somewhere higher like the upper floors of your home. Don't take shelter in the basement as your home may take in water and the flooding will hit the lowest areas of your house. In some cases, desperate people during an intense storm surge take shelter on the roof of their homes.

- Avoid power lines and electrical lines. You may be electrocuted easily because water is an excellent conductor of electricity. If you see electrical wires, steer clear of them.

- Don't try to swim through the flood. The current may grow stronger and you may get washed away and you may even drown if you're not careful enough.

- If the flood is about the level of your ankles, don't go any further and find another way through. This much water is more than enough to knock your off your feet and wash you away.

- If you have to, evacuate your area immediately. Get to the local safe zones designated by the local authorities to ensure your safety. Get your emergency bug out bag and head there immediately. If you think that your home can't handle a flood, go to the shelter in advance.

- If the flood manages to reach your home, shut off your electricity and unplug all of your electrical appliances. If you can, take all of your electrical appliances to the upper floors of your home away from the flood so that they don't get damaged by the water. This reduces the risk of you getting electrocuted in your own home and it might just save your life.

Conclusion - The Aftermath Of A Disaster

And there you have it. A disaster is a stressful event in anyone's life. Anyone can get scared or anxious when a disaster occurs, but keeping a composed mind and having the proper knowledge on what to do during a disaster is a must. The preparation phase for a disaster also places of equal importance since it makes you ready and allows you to save time and effort by doing the things that you need to do during a disaster beforehand.

But what about after a disaster? Here are the things that you should take note and the things that you should do after a disaster occurs.

- Don't panic! Survey the safety of your area and see if you can safely navigate through the area. This is especially true after an earthquake since a lot of people get trapped indoors and the risk of aftershocks endangers the lives of many.

- Contact 911 or your local emergency hotline immediately to let them know of your situation. If you are trapped, all the more reason to call them.

- Call your family and loved ones. Start contacting them one by one if you can to ensure their safety and to survey other areas affected by the disaster.

- Turn off electrical power or gas lines to ensure that even worse situations won't rise from the aftermath of a disaster.

- Once you've assured that everything is safe, it's time to start cleaning up.